The Rockwool Foundation Research Unit

Study Paper No. 74

Sharing The Fire

The igniting role of transformational leadership
on the relationship between public managers' and
employees' organizational commitment

Camilla Denager Staniok and
Christian Bøtcher Jacobsen

University Press of Southern Denmark

Odense 2014

Sharing The Fire

The igniting role of transformational leadership on the relationship between public managers' and employees' organizational commitment

Study Paper No. 74

Published by:
© The Rockwool Foundation Research Unit

Address:
The Rockwool Foundation Research Unit
Soelvgade 10, 2.tv.
DK-1307 Copenhagen K

Telephone	+45 33 34 48 00
E-mail	forskningsenheden@rff.dk
web site:	www.en.rff.dk

ISBN 978-87-93119-16-1
ISSN 0908-3979

August 2014

ABSTRACT

Seminal articles on organizational commitment in public organizations have assumed that employees reciprocate the attitudes of their peers, but recent studies suggest that the impact of managers' organizational commitment on employees' organizational commitment depends on *how* leaders convey their organizational commitment. In this study we investigate how *transformational leadership* moderates the relationship between mangers' and employees' organizational commitment. Multilevel data from surveys of 68 principals and 1,349 teachers in the area of upper secondary education show that there is no direct relationship between principals' and teachers' organizational commitment, but that transformational leadership moderates the relationship. Only if a principal is seen as transformational, his organizational commitment is positively related to the employees' organizational commitment, but if he is seen as non-transformational, the relationship is negative. Thus, managers are much more able to convey their organizational commitment, when they are transformational.

INTRODUCTION

Research from the past several decades suggests that public managers should take their employees' affective organizational commitment as a central concern, because it can be an effective tool to improve public employee retention and performance (Porter et al., 1976; Mowday et al., 1979; Meyer et al. 2002; Steinhaus & Perry, 1996; Wright & Bonett, 2002; Park & Rainey, 2007). Often managers are assumed to play key roles for the affective organizational commitment of the employees, as employees expectedly reciprocate the attitudes of their peers (Hambrick & Mason, 1984; Stevens et al., 1978). Seminal contributions within the field of organizational commitment *theorize* that public employees' affective organizational commitment can be expected to emanate from interpersonal influences of peers and organizational socialization (e.g. Stevens et al., 1978). From a top-down perspective, managers have a strong influence on the development and institutionalization of the organizational culture due to their formally assigned authority and power within public organizations, and thus the attitudes of the employees (Rainey & Steinbauer, 1999; Scott, 2008). From a bottom-up perspective employees seek legitimacy and acknowledgement and are therefore likely to copy attitudes known to be successful and/or professionally recognized - such as the one of the manager (Christensen et al., 2009: 130-147). Accordingly, employees' affective organizational commitment can be expected to reflect the affective organizational commitment of the manager. However, the relationship between managers' and employees' affective organizational commitment remains surprisingly neglected in empirical studies (Meyer et al., 2002; Solinger et al., 2008). This leaves us with the critical question of, *how* managers can convey their affective organizational commitment to their followers?

Recent contributions within the literature focus on the institutional context in which public organizations are embedded (Stazyk et al., 2011; Park & Rainey, 2007). They emphasize the potential negative impact of goal ambiguity, lack of involvement and excessive red tape have on organizational commitment in the public sector (Rainey, 2009; Stazyk et al., 2011; Park & Rainey, 2007).

Goal ambiguity and deleterious bureaucracy have long been known to cause severe challenges for managers in ensuring that employees work in the same direction and commit to shared purposes and beliefs (Wilson, 1989; Bozeman, 2000). Organizationally committed managers in public organizations, who have a strong focus on sharing their vision for the organization and clarifying the mission, can therefore, be expected to be better at overcoming the constraining and ambiguous environment and communicate their affective organizational commitment to the employees (Oberfield, 2012; Wright et al., 2012). A long body of research confirms that a transformational leadership style clarifies the goals and vision of the organization, and supports and inspires employees in their work processes (Wright et al., 2012). Several studies have also empirically documented positive relationships between transformational leadership style and a range of different work attitudes including organizational commitment (see e.g. Bass & Riggio 2006; Dumdum et al., 2002; Trottier et al., 2008). However, these studies focus exclusively on managers' transformational leadership style and employees' organizational commitment and neglect mangers' organizational commitment. Thus, the literature may have overlooked the potentially important interplay between both managers' and employees' organizational commitment and leadership style.

In sum, there is a need for greater attention to *how* public managers can convey their affective organizational commitment to their followers in order to develop a more complete and empirical understanding of the interpersonal workings of affective organizational commitment in the environment of the public sector.

The purpose of the present paper is to study the relationship between public managers' and employees' affective organizational commitment taking into account managers' transformational leadership style. To do so, it draws on previously established conceptions of affective organizational commitment and transformational leadership. More specifically the relationship between managers' and employees' affective organizational commitment is investigated empirically in the area of upper secondary education in Denmark. This is a well-suited area, because the employees refer to one manager in well-defined organizations with more or less identical services and goals. The study is based on two electronic surveys of 68 managers and 1,349 teachers, which provides an unusual opportunity to study relationships between organizational commitment and leadership style in a multi-level setup at manager and employee levels.

Hence, this paper contributes to the vast literature on organizational commitment by testing one of the early and underlying propositions of peer influences on a unique dataset. More generally the study adds to our knowledge on, *how* managers can influence public employees' work-related attitudes. In the next section we present the theoretical framework and our two main hypotheses. This is followed by a description of the data and methods, and a presentation of the results. Finally, we discuss the results, conclude and point towards further research.

THEORETICAL FRAMEWORK

Affective organizational commitment

The enduring and multidisciplinary interest in organizational commitment has resulted in an immense literature and a myriad of different approaches (Angle & Perry, 1981; Balfour & Wechsler, 1996; Mathieu & Zajac, 1990; Cohen, 2003; Meyer et al., 2002). Generally, some studies conceptualize organizational commitment as an attitude (e.g. Mowday et al., 1979, Porter et al., 1976) and others as a behavior (O'Reilly & Caldwell, 1980; Kline & Peters, 1991). Moreover, some studies argue that organizational commitment is a uni-dimensional concept (e.g. Mathieu and Zajac, Angle and Perry, 1981; 1990; Sollinger et al., 2008) while others argue that commitment consists of several dimensions (e.g. Meyer & Allen, 1991, 1997; Meyer, Allen & Smith, 1993). In this paper we conceptualize organizational commitment exclusively as *affective* organizational commitment. Drawing on both on early attitudinal contributions as well as the established framework of Meyer and Allen (1991; 1997) affective organizational commitment is defined as: 'as an emotional attachment to, identification with, and involvement in an organization' (Porter et al.,

1976). Previous studies have shown that affective organizational commitment is the type of commitment that has proved to be most strongly related to organizational issues and employee-related attitudes and behavior (see e.g. the meta-analysis by Meyer et al., 2002). Furthermore, as our primary interest is in assessing organizational commitment empirically we rely on Meyer and Allen's conceptualization of affective organizational commitment, which is by far the most used and validated approach in empirical studies of organizational commitment (Sollinger et a., 2008; Klein et al., 2012). More concrete, Meyer and Allen argue that affective organizational commitment develops when an individual becomes involved in, recognizes the value-relevance of and/or derives his or her identity from an organization (Meyer et al., 2001; 316-317). Employees with a strong affective commitment thus remain with the organization because they *want* to and not because they feel they need or ought to (Meyer et al., 1993).

Following this brief definition of organizational commitment we will discuss the most relevant studies of organizational commitment in public organizations and in continuation hereof present the core hypotheses of this paper. The discussion is structured in two parts. The first part concerns the link between managers' and employees' affective organizational commitment whereas the second part concerns the relationship between transformational leadership style and organizational commitment.

Managers' and employees' affective organizational commitment

Managers are often assumed to have a crucial influence on employees' perceptual evaluations (Hambrick & Mason, 1984; Rainey, 2009). Both in the more generic management literature as well as in the fields of public administration and organizational behavior this profound assumption is an important building block for theories of work motivation and leadership (Wilson, 1989; Christensen et al, 2008; Scott; 2008; Rainey & Steinbauer, 1999; Meier & O'Toole, 2011). Also several studies of organizational commitment rely on this theoretical assumption. For instance Stevens, Beyer and Trice note in their early work that organizational commitment can: 'be expected to emanate from interpersonal influences of peers and organizational socialization' (Stevens et al., 1978: 393). Similarly, Klein, Molloy and Brinsfeld (2012) recently argued that: 'individuals' professional and personal relationships yield social exchanges and social influences that facilitate the formation of commitment bonds' (Klein et al., 2012:141-142).

The assumption of interpersonal effects of organizational commitment between managers and employees finds support in both bottom-up as well as top-down perspectives. The two perspectives differ in their focus of attention, but both provide support for the expectation that managers' organizational commitment have an important influence on employees' organizational commitment.

Top-down perspectives center on the organizational culture and the impact that managers have on employees' work attitudes through the development and institutionalization of the organizational culture (Rainey & Steinbauer, 1999; Scott, 2008). Organizational culture is probably one of the most overused (and misused) concepts in contemporary management studies, but nonetheless an important factor in many public management studies (Schein, 1992; Christensen et al. 2008). We understand organizational culture as patterns of shared meaning in organizations including shared values and beliefs about appropriate behaviors and actions (Smircich, 1983: 58; Scott, 2008). Organizational culture manifests itself and is influenced by symbols, ceremonies, statements and actions of the manager (Rainey, 1999; Scott, 2008). In this context, organizational culture is perceived as a variable, meaning something the organization has and not as something the organization is (Schein, 1992). Furthermore organizational culture is seen as representing a collective social construction over which managers have substantial control. In other words, managers are expected to have salient positions in developing, transforming, and institutionalizing organizational cultures (Rainey & Steinbauer, 1999; Scott, 2008). According to classic institutional and organizational theory managers who signal a high commitment to the organization increase the internal integration within the organization, because managers thereby provide employees with guidelines to choose appropriate activities and a source of meaning and identification (Scott & Davis, 2007: 212-215; Selznick, 1948: 125). Managers can signal commitment to the organization through for instance goal setting or formulation of local policies (Scott & Davis, 2007: 212-215). Managers' organizational commitment can therefore be expected to strengthen or sustain strong organizational cultures and hence to affect the organizational commitment of the employees.

Bottom-up perspectives in favor of the argument that employees' affective organizational commitment is affected by the mangers' affective organizational commitment centers on the concept of legitimacy and find their support in institutional theory, role model theory and theory on peer effects (Scott, 2008; Summers & Wolfe, 1977; Henderson et al., 1978; Argys et al., 1996). Legitimacy can be defined as a generalized perception or assumption of desirable, proper, or appropriate actions or attitudes within a socially constructed system of norms, values, and beliefs (definition inspired by Suchman, 1995: 574). Employees seek legitimacy and acknowledgement and are therefore likely to copy attitudes known to be successful and/or professionally recognized, or adapt to the prevailing "logic of appropriateness" (Scott, 2008: 58-60; Christensen et al., 2009: 130-147). According to Scott, individuals align themselves with prevailing cultural beliefs because it makes them feel competent and connected (Scott, 2008: 50). Likewise Meyer & Rowan (1977) emphasize the extent to which wider belief systems and cultural frames are imposed and or adopted by individuals (Meyer & Rowan, 1977). The expectation is therefore, that the managers serve as role models of legitimate behavior and attitudes for the employees. By setting a high work standard and expressing a strong morale and determination to reach the goals of the organization managers challenge, encourage or inspire the employees to assume greater ownership of their work attitude and strengthen their organizational commitment (Wright et al., 2012).

Summing up the discussions above we propose the following hypothesis:

Hypothesis 1: There is a positive relationship between public managers' affective organizational commitment and employees' affective organizational commitment

Organizational commitment and transformational leadership

External forces and political principals have a strong influence on public organizations' internal structures and processes (Wilson, 1989; Chun & Rainey, 2005; Latham et al., 2008; Wright, 2004) and scholars of organizational commitment in the public sector argue that public managers face particular challenges due to the institutional context in which they are embedded, (Stazyk et al, 2011; Park & Rainey, 2007; Rainey, 2009: 312). Stazyk, Pandey & Wright (2011) propose and test a model of affective organizational commitment that integrates specific institutional characteristics of public organizations. The analyses show that goal ambiguity and red tape have a negative impact on employees' organizational commitment. Similarly, Park and Rainey (2007) find that organizational commitment in federal agencies among other factors is strongly related to public institutional characteristics such as lack of involvement and goal clarity (Park & Rainey, 2007). Following these studies, we argue that, because goal ambiguity, low levels of employee involvement and excessive red tape are critical factors in public organizations that affect organizational commitment, public managers' transformational leadership style is of great importance. Goal ambiguity, red tape and lack of involvement can in other words be said to prescribe a management attitude that take into account the impacts these institutional factors potentially have on employees' work attitudes.

Transformational leadership is often defined in opposition or relation to its transactional counterpart (Burns, 1978; Bass, 1985). According to Bass the transactional leader practices contingent reinforcement of followers whereas the transformational leader inspires, intellectually stimulates, and individually considerate them (Bass, 1990). Moreover, transformational leaders motivate followers to transcend their own narrow self-interest for the benefit of the community and thus lift followers' focus from lower- to higher-order needs (Avolio et al., 2004). A transformational leadership style can theoretically be expected to have crucial impact on the relationship between public managers' and employees' affective organizational commitment because: 1) it clarifies the goals and privileges the mission of the organization, 2) it engages follower in recognizing and confronting work-related challenges, and 3) it coaches and supports followers in their work processes (Rainey, 2009: 325-331). These transformational leadership traits can directly be linked to the abovementioned challenges that public managers are facing and thus to mediate the relationship between managerial and employee commitment.

First of all, because public organizations by definition are meant to consider and satisfy different democratic and public issues of society public managers are constantly confronted with changing political priorities among inconsistent organizational goals (Perry & Rainey, 1988). Organizationally committed public managers with a strong focus on sharing their vision for the organization and clarifying the goals and mission can therefore be expected to be better at communicating their involvement and emotional concern about the organization to their followers. (Avolio et al., 2004; Wright et al., 2012). On the contrary public managers without a transformational leadership style can be expected to signal a distance to the organizational goals and mission.

Secondly, early studies by Buchanan (1974) have shown that members of public organizations can be expected to express low levels of job involvement, when they feel they only have little impact on the large and complex system in which they take part (Buchanan, 1974). Organizationally committed managers with a transformational leadership style focus on engaging their followers by intellectually stimulating them to challenge old assumptions about organizational problems and practices, and can thus be expected to have more success in sharing their organizational commitment. On the contrary public managers, who do not have a transformational leadership style can be expected to fail to engage employees in recognizing and confronting challenges and in viewing their job from different perspectives (Bass 1985, 1990). Balfour and Wechsler's study from 1996 support this argument. They report that especially participation and supportive supervision had a positive influence on employees' organizational commitment (Balfour & Wechsler, 1996).

Finally, exacerbated efforts in public organizations to maintain or increase coordination and accountability often result in rule proliferation and hierarchy (Stazyk & Goerdel, 2011; Warwick et al., 1975). Unfortunately, the promulgation of rules intended to ensure coordination and accountability frequently reflects public organizations' multiple external stakeholders and often results in excessive red tape (Bozeman, 2000). Red tape may challenge managers in communicating the vision and mission of the organization (Stazyk &, 2011). Several studies have found red tape or inevitable bureaucracy to have significant negative effects on employees' organizational commitment, motivation, job-satisfaction as well as other work-related attitudes (see e.g. Bozeman, 200; Pandey & Rainey, 2006; Stazyk et al., 2011). Organizational committed managers who focus on coaching and supporting their employees' through a transformational leadership style can therefore be expected to be better at accentuating the core values and vision of the organization. On the contrary mangers without a transformational leadership style can be expected let the power arrangement reflected in the procurement systems inundate their managerial visions for the organization and overshadow their organizational engagement.

In sum a transformational leadership style is expected to affect *how* mangers affective organizational commitment affect employees' organizational commitment, because it facilitates managers' communication of the organizational values and goals thereby supporting employees emotional attachment to, identification with, and involvement in an organization. Managerial organizational commitment is all about wishing to achieve the organizational goals and feeling a sense of connectedness to organization. Transformational leadership is all about communicating it. On that background we hypothesize as follows:

Hypothesis 2: School principals' affective organizational commitment is more positively related to their employees' affective organizational commitment, the more the managers are perceived to exert transformational leadership style.

RESEARCH DESIGN

As argued above we have numerous studies on organizational commitment, but we still know relatively little about the impact of managers' organizational commitment on employees' organizational commitment in the public sector. To investigate this relationship empirically, this study focuses on Danish upper secondary schools (publicly owned and funded), because this area provides at least four advantages. First, we can relatively easily link employees with their manager, since all school principals are responsible for personnel management for all teachers at the schools. Second, Danish upper secondary schools are very similar, because they produce more or less identical services, and this allows us to keep a number of potentially disturbing variables constant. Third, a recent reform in this area has allowed the principals much more power and autonomy, which provides them better opportunities to actively exert their leadership. Fourth and finally, simultaneously gathered survey data is available for school principals and teachers respectively. This allows us to use a multilevel design, so we can control for a number of unobserved school level variables. We will discuss data in further detail below. Next section shortly introduces the Danish school system and elaborates on the advantages introduced above.

In the Danish school system, the first ten years of basic schooling (*grundskole*) are mandatory (grades 0 through 9), and after graduation students are obliged to continue their education in either a vocational or a general direction. This study focuses on the largest general education, STX, which provide nationally regulated, tuition-free, general education to almost half of the Danish youth (around 42.000 students in 2010 according to The Ministry of Children and Education, 2010). Traditionally, these schools have functioned in a hierarchical setting, but following a recent reform in 2007, the schools obtained substantially more autonomy and are now self-governing with their own supervisory boards and financed through activity-based budgeting (based on the number of students enrolled and passing exams). Thus, school principals are now in a much better position to exert their leadership than they used to be.

The schools all have a relatively flat structure with short distance from principal to the teachers. Thus, most principals have personnel management responsibility for all teachers, and most of them engage on a daily basis with the teachers. The principal is therefore a main character at the school, and to a large extent personify the school management. Though middle management probably takes up more resources than earlier, the tasks of middle managers are mainly administrative, whereas personnel management primarily remains with the principals. On this background there is good reason to expect that principals can exert influence on their teachers.

DATA

We have approached all 135 STX schools in Denmark with an invitation to participate in two parallel surveys directed at the managerial level and the employee level respectively. In October 2012 we sent a letter to the school, where we requested contact information for all managers (principals and middle managers) and teachers. Most schools sent us the information, and for most other schools, we were able to gather information from their websites. Nine schools were left out of the investigation either because they actively refused to participate, or because we could not obtain contact information. In late November, we sent web-based questionnaires to 135 principals and 8,600 teachers, and throughout December we sent four reminders to those, who had not yet responded. When the survey was closed on December 21st, 76 principals and 2,934 teachers (response rates 60.3 percent and 34.1 percent respectively) had completed the survey. 68 principal responses were complete, and we use these and the 1,349 teachers at these schools in the analyses below.

MEASURES

All variables in the study were measured in a multilevel setup using responses from multiple survey items from both teachers and principals. The surveys were set up to measure a number of identical variables, which allows us a multilevel dataset, where we can couple teacher and principal responses into the same dataset. Some items vary slightly, so they fit with the relevant type of respondent (e.g. leadership style, which were opened with either 'As a leader I…' or 'My leader…'). All items have been taken from previously validated and commonly used measures. We have translated all items to English and back again to validate the content of the items, and before the actual survey we ran a pilot study to 150 teachers and one principal, which resulted in a somewhat extensive adjustment of the survey. Primarily, the survey was shortened, but also the wording of some items was changed. The main variables in the dataset are organizational commitment and transformative leadership, which are measured among both teachers and principals. Also we include a number of control variables, including transactional leadership (reward and exception respectively). Organizational commitment was measured with two items taken from Meyer & Allen (1993; 1997), which reflect affective commitment to the organization. Both items have a negative wording, and they have therefore been reversed. The factor loadings among both teachers and principals are slightly below the recommended 0.7, but the reliability of the scale at both levels turn out very satisfactory. Transformational leadership is measured with four items taken from Podsakoff et al. (1993), Trottier et al. (2008), and Wright et al. (2012), which reflect both visionary leadership and inspirational leadership style. Generally, our attempts to replicate scales from these other studies failed, so we have used a new scale building on items from different studies. Nonetheless, we argue that both the content validity of these items are high, and the factor analysis is also highly satisfactory with loadings around 0.80 for teachers and 0.7 for principals (except one item among principals). We will return to this point in the discussion section.

Table 1: Sample characteristics ($n_{principals}$ = 68, $n_{teachers}$ = 1.349)

	M	SD	Min	Max
School level				
Principal organizational commitment	82.57	23.18	25	100
Principal age	57.92	6.53	42	69
Principal gender (female = 1)	0.26	0.44	0	1
Principal's tenure (years, current school)	11.52	7.53	0	31
School size (no. of teachers)	81.08	20.02	38	137
Teacher level				
Teacher organizational commitment	70.04	25.40	0	100
Teacher transformational leadership	51.07	24.97	0	100
Teacher management by reward	37.30	25.86	0	100
Teacher management by exception	32.83	22.46	0	100
Age	44.84	11.52	24	71
Gender (female = 1)	0.52	0.50	0	1
Tenure (years, current school)	11.50	11.05	0	48
Teaching area (science = 1)	0.25	0.44	0	1

Regarding control variables, the items measuring transactional leadership style (management by reward and management by exception respectively) were taken from Trottier et al. (2008) and Den Hartog et al. (1997), and among both teachers and principals we find strong factors for management by reward (loadings around 0.7) and a weaker factor for management by exception (loadings below 0.6). Table 1 shows the summary statistics of both explanatory and control variables, which are mainly self-reported in the survey, including age, gender, and tenure (general and organizational). From the teacher survey, we have gathered information on the teachers' subjects, which we have coded into broad areas (science or non-science). The number of teachers is gathered from our lists of respondents, which cover all teachers at each school.

We expect age to be positively correlated with organizational commitment, because experience will typically bring individual and organization closer together (Hrebiniak & Alutto, 1972). However, much of this effect has to do with organizational experience, so we also control for organizational tenure. We also control for gender with the expectation that women will be more organizational committed than their male counterparts. However, according to Mathieu and Zajac (1990) research on gender and organizational commitment is inconclusive. Some studies report that women are more committed than men (e.g. Angle and Perry, 1981), some suggest that women are less committed than men (e.g. Aranya et al, 1986 and Chusmir, 1982), and others report no gender differences (e.g. Fry & Grenfeld, 1980 and Stevens, Beyer and Trice, 1978). At the teacher level, we also control for teaching area, because we expect non-science teachers to be more emotional and therefore potentially more affectively committed to the organization.

Furthermore, a number of school level characteristics related to both the school and the principal can be important for organizational commitment. Regarding leader characteristics we control for gender, age, and tenure in the current position. The literature offers few findings on these aspects, so we include them mainly for control purposes. We also control for school size (number of teachers), and expect organizational commitment to be negatively related to organization size (Dekker & Barling, 1995). Descriptive statistics and correlations regarding all variables, including indexes measuring organizational commitment and leadership styles can be seen from Table A1.

METHODS

As mentioned, the dataset has a multilevel structure. The unit of analysis is the teacher, so we have identified principals and merged our principal and teacher datasets into one. All analyses are run as random effects models. To check the robustness of the results, we have replicated our findings using OLS regression with cluster robust standard errors, but since the results are highly similar, we only show the estimates from the multilevel models, which we find to be more correctly specified. We are confident in the choice of random effects model after we have run an "empty" multilevel model to test whether auto-correlation is a problem in our data. When we omit the explanatory variables in the "empty" model, only the variance of the dependent variable, the teachers' organizational commitment, is being investigated. The "empty" model shows that there is significant variation between schools, which indicates that a random effects model is appropriate. The random effects also show that there is more variation within schools than between schools, suggesting that individual factors are more important than school factors in explaining differences in the teachers' organizational commitment. Even though there is more variation within schools than between schools, the empty model confirms that school factors are important, and hence that principals' leadership style and organizational commitment can be important for the teachers' organizational commitment. Following these findings from the "empty" model, all other analyses include random effects to control for schools effects.

RESULTS

This section presents results from a series of multi-level models investigating the relationship between transformational leadership and principals' and teachers' organizational commitment controlled for a number of variables at both organizational and individual level. Model 1 tests the relationship between the control variables and the teachers' organizational commitment. Hypothesis 1 is tested in model 2, which show analyses of the association between the principals' organizational commitment and teachers' organizational commitment. Hypotheses 2 is tested in model 3, 4 and 5, which shows the same relationships including employees' perceived transformational leadership style, an interaction term between the principal's organizational commitment and how teacher's perceive the principals transformational leadership style, and a number of other control variables.

Model 1 (table 2) shows that only some control variables are related to the teachers' organizational commitment. Teachers' age and tenure are not surprisingly correlated, but it is interesting to see, how they are oppositely related with commitment. The correlation with age is negative, whereas the correlation with tenure is positive. Tenure is potentially highly endogenous to commitment, since highly committed teachers are probably more likely to stay in their current job. Female teachers have markedly higher organizational commitment than male teachers. At the school level, only the principal's gender makes a difference for the teachers' organizational commitment, and surprisingly this relationship is negative.

Model 2 shows that the principal's organizational commitment has no significant relationship with the teachers' organizational commitment. Thus, we must reject hypothesis 1. Model 3 shows that this does not change, when we control for the teachers' perception of the principal's transformational leadership style. Only the transformational leadership variable is positively related to organizational commitment. In model 4 the interaction term between the principal's organizational commitment and the teachers' perception of transformational leadership style is introduced for a test of hypothesis 2. The interaction term shows a significant, positive relationship, meaning that principals' organizational commitment and teacher perceived transformational leadership enhance each other's positive relationship with the teachers' organizational commitment. Based on this, we accept hypothesis 2. To test the robustness of this finding, we do, nonetheless, control for other leadership behaviors, since it has been argued that transformational and transactional leadership styles are cumulative rather than mutually exclusive (Bass, 1990). Hence, we may be overestimating the explanatory power of transformational leadership. In model 5 two measures of employee perceived transactional leadership behaviors are introduced (management by reward and management by exception), and both of these are significantly related with organizational commitment, though in opposite directions. Teachers who perceive their managers to be rewarding have higher commitment, whereas teachers who perceive their managers to exert management by exception, report lower commitment. Most importantly, we see that the interaction is left unchanged by this control. Only transformational leadership style becomes insignificant.

Building on the logic of the interaction analysis, we can depict the relationship between principals' organizational commitment and the teachers' organizational commitment for extreme values of transformational leadership (Figure 1). The figure shows that when principals are perceived as having a high degree of transformational leadership (the red line), the principal's organizational commitment is positively related with the teacher's organizational commitment. However, when a principal is not seen as transformational (the blue line), his organizational commitment affects the teacher's organizational commitment negatively. We will discuss this is further detail below.

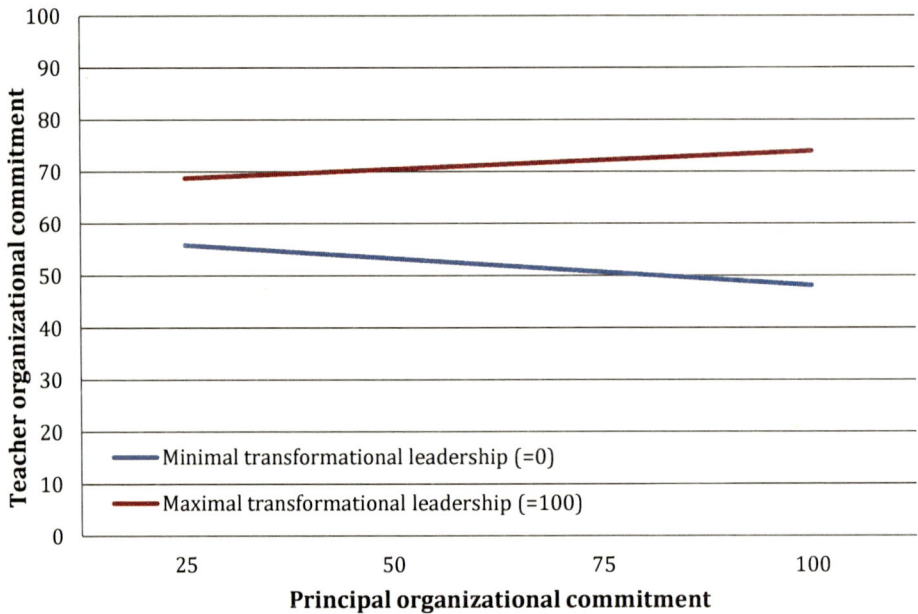

As a final remark on the results, the analyses show that the relationships of the control variables are generally strengthened, when we take the explanatory variables into consideration. Thus, model 5 shows that age and tenure remain significant and oppositely related to commitment, and the finding that women have higher organizational commitment is consistent across the models. Model 5 shows that science teachers have lower commitment, and so do part time workers. The principal's age and tenure are significantly related to organizational commitment in model 5, and as we saw at the teacher level, the coefficients are in opposite directions. However, the directions are opposite compared to the teachers' own age and tenure, meaning that principal age is positively related, whereas principal tenure is negatively related to teacher organizational commitment. Finally, we see that teachers with female principals consistently report lower organizational commitment, and that school size becomes significantly, negatively related to organizational commitment in model 3 and onwards.

The r-squared statistics show how much of the variation between and within schools the models explain. The models generally explain more of the variation between schools than within schools, but still we are able to explain 16.2 percent of the variation within schools and 33.8 percent of the variation between schools in our final model. The robustness of our results has been tested in several ways. First, we have tried using different operationalizations of the dependent variable. Besides using a sum index, we have used factor loadings and tried different specifications of the items. Second, we have tried different estimation techniques, as we have also tested the five models with OLS regression with cluster robust standard errors. None of these approaches changed our results.

Table 2. Multilevel regression of employee organizational commitment (oce). (Random effects, unstandardized regression, t stats in parentheses)

Var name	Var label	'Empty' model	Model 1	Model 2	Model 3	Model 4	Model 5
poc	Principal organizational commitment (p)		0.0192 (0.52)	-0.0503 (-1.54)	-0.312** (-3.34)	-0.162** (-2.68)	-0.160** (-2.65)
ttl	Transformational leadership (t)			0.375*** (13.69)		0.184* (2.37)	0.115 (1.48)
int	Interaction, ocm*tle (p*t)					0.00236* (2.47)	0.00231* (2.44)
trl	Management by reward (t)						0.102*** (3.75)
tel	Management by exception (t)						-0.0897** (-2.73)
Teacher level control variables							
tag	Age (years)		-0.304** (-2.99)	-0.302** (-2.97)	-0.311*** (-3.34)	-0.311*** (-3.30)	-0.336*** (-3.52)
tge	Gender (female=1)		4.559*** (3.57)	4.548*** (3.55)	3.841** (3.01)	3.780** (2.97)	3.509** (2.76)
tte	Tenure, current job (years)		0.479*** (4.40)	0.477*** (4.34)	0.552*** (5.73)	0.548*** (5.59)	0.558*** (5.60)
tta	Teaching area (science = 1, other = 0)		-3.447 (-1.95)	-3.455 (-1.95)	-3.792* (-2.33)	-3.877* (-2.43)	-3.853* (-2.41)
tpw	Part time		-2.966 (-1.66)	-2.955 (-1.65)	-4.763** (-2.86)	-4.689** (-2.83)	-4.670** (-2.88)
School level control variables							
pag	Principal age (years)		0.327 (1.73)	0.327 (1.74)	0.481** (3.03)	0.482** (3.10)	0.499** (3.20)
pte	Principal tenure, current job (years)		-0.288* (-2.49)	-0.288* (-2.43)	-0.381** (-3.29)	-0.364** (-3.04)	-0.352** (-3.09)
Pge	Principal gender (female=1)		-2.724 (-1.23)	-2.883 (-1.32)	-4.106* (-2.27)	-4.213* (-2.41)	-3.946* (-2.27)
Siz	School size (no. of teachers)		-0.0475 (-1.26)	-0.0497 (-1.30)	-0.0762** (-2.68)	-0.0692* (-2.44)	-0.0722* (-2.56)
Con	Constant	70.56*** (82.92)	66.65*** (5.73)	65.17*** (5.70)	46.72*** (5.01)	54.71*** (5.35)	57.63*** (5.51)
n	Observations (teachers)	1,349	1,349	1,349	1,349	1,349	1,349
	Groups (schools)	68	68	68	68	68	68
R^2	Within	0.0000	0.0298	0.0298	0.1467	0.1485	0.1615
	Between	0.0000	0.1267	0.1300	0.3186	0.3317	0.3395
	Overall	0.0000	0.0361	0.0364	0.1614	0.1646	0.1779
Sigma_u		4.0126	4.0305	4.1234	3.0242	2.9382	3.1633
Sigma_e		25.0038	24.6758	24.6758	23.1495	23.1332	22.9719
Rho		0.02511	0.02599	0.02717	0.01678	0.001588	0.01861

Note: (t): teacher level, (p): principal level, * $p < 0.05$, ** $p < 0.01$, *** $p < 0.00$

DISCUSSION AND CONCLUSION

Using multilevel survey data from Danish principals and teachers in the area of upper secondary education, this study set out to investigate the link between managers' and employees' organizational commitment taking the principals' transformational leadership style into account. Our results provide support for one of the hypotheses we have set forward. According to our results the principal's organizational commitment is not directly significantly related to the teachers' organizational commitment, so we reject hypothesis 1. However, this relationship changes when we control for the teachers' perception of the principal's transformational leadership style, so the more a teacher perceives that the principal exerts transformational leadership behavior, the more positively the principal's organizational commitment is related to the teacher's organizational commitment. These findings thereby lend support to hypothesis 2.

Regarding the rejection of hypothesis 1, this finding theoretically contradicts our initial expectations. Managers were expected to affect their followers through the organization culture due to their formally assigned authority (Rainey & Steinbauer, 1999) and by serving as strong role models inspiring and encouraging employees (Wright et al., 2012). These results though show that employees do not per se mirror the attitudes of their manager (Hambrick & Mason, 1984; Stevens et al., 1978). Instead our analyses clearly suggest, that principals' transformational leadership style, measured as teachers' perceptions, moderate the relationship between principal and employee commitment. Results thus confirm that there is an important interplay between transformational leadership style and principals' and teachers' organizational commitment, which so far have been overlooked.

This study should be considered in view of certain issues and limitations. First, though we have based the survey on validated scales, we had difficulties replicating the factor structures found elsewhere. We can only speculate on whether this is due to specific Danish characteristics or characteristics of the Danish education sector. Nonetheless, the reader should be aware of the disparities between our measurements and those seen elsewhere. Second, although the multilevel data structure applied here has provided a rare opportunity for combining measurements of manager and employee organizational commitment, we still know very little about the causal relationships between commitment and leadership. Thus, it could be argued that the direction of causality is reverse, and that managers' organizational commitment are affected by their employees organizational commitment, or that transformational leadership style is the actual explanatory variable and managers' organizational commitment the moderating variable. Since organizational commitment is difficult to manipulate in experimental set-ups, a palpable strategy could be to obtain panel data over time in order to study how organizational commitment and leadership style develop over time and between managers and employees. Third, and to follow up on the second notion, it would be relevant to see similar studies on other occupations and sectors than the teaching area to test the wider applicability of the findings. The results are very likely to be relevant for other areas. Though, we have no statistical background for claiming this, we can from analytical purposes suggest that the results should be seen as very relevant for the teaching area in general. Since the Danish upper secondary schools are rather similar to for example the American high schools (Christensen & Pallesen, 2009), the results are likely to have some broader international relevance.

Summing up, the main contribution of this study is to show organizationally committed may in fact convey their organizational commitment to their employees, but only if they apply a transformational leadership style. Furthermore, the study suggests that the combination of measurements of organizational commitment and leadership styles measured at different levels is useful for providing more nuanced answer for fundamental questions within the literature. An important implication can be deduced from our findings. So far the literature has suggested that transformational leadership spurs organizational commitment, but we suggest that this relationship is more complicated than so. We have shown that the relationship depends on the manager's organizational commitment, and on theoretical grounds we suggest that transformational leadership clarifies and attenuates the leaders' commitment. Being organizationally committed to the organization does not do it alone, if managers are interested in fostering commitment among their employees. But adjusting the style of leadership towards a more transformational leadership behavior is not likely to work, if the employees do not sense a commitment to the organization. Focusing on the interactions between organizational commitment and leadership style seems to be a fruitful avenue for further research, but we also need more studies to help untangle the complex relationships between these variables. As for now, all we can say is that managers may share their fire with the employees, but they should be aware of *how* they do it.

Table A1. Correlation Information

	(1)	(2)	(3)	(4)	(5)	(6)	(7)	(8)	(9)	(10)	(11)	(12)	(13)	(14)
(1) Org. commitment (t)	1.000													
(2) Org. commitment (p)	0.014	1.000												
(3) Transform. leadership (trl) (t)	0.329***	0.178***	1.000											
(4) Interaction, ocp*tlt	0.283***	0.577***	0.873***	1.000										
(5) Man. by reward (mbr) (t)	0.218***	0.104***	0.449***	0.402***	1.000									
(6) Man. by exception (mbe) (t)	-0.184***	-0.030	-0.309***	-0.263***	-0.090***	1.000								
Teacher level control variables														
(7) Age	0.012	-0.016	-0.062*	-0.052	0.028	-0.000	1.000							
(8) Gender (female=1)	0.092***	0.015	0.050	0.049	0.015	-0.090***	-0.113***	1.000						
(9) Tenure, current job	0.076**	0.018	-0.079**	-0.049	-0.001	0.012	0.813***	-0.117***	1.000					
(10) Teaching area (science = 1, other = 0)	-0.082**	0.016	0.014	0.024	0.028	0.017	0.052	-0.146***	0.027	1.000				
(11) Part time	-0.043	-0.008	0.064*	0.045	0.050	0.005	0.102***	0.014	0.075**	0.029	1.000			
School level control variables														
(12) Principal age	0.021	-0.034	-0.060*	-0.083**	-0.015	0.119***	-0.046	-0.008	-0.059*	-0.028	0.018	1.000		
(13) Principal gender (female=1)	-0.042	0.156	0.085**	0.148***	0.059*	0.053	-0.017	-0.017	-0.019	0.007	0.023	-0.104***	1.000	
(14) Principal tenure, current job	-0.027	-0.035***	-0.011	-0.051	0.027	0.129***	-0.038	-0.024	-0.021	0.003	-0.014	0.676***	-0.163***	1.000
(15) School size (no. of teachers)	-0.025	0.085**	0.059*	0.060*	0.088**	0.041	-0.029	0.030	-0.028	0.025	-0.067*	0.116***	-0.019	0.050

Note: Correlations (Pearson's r). (t): employee level, (p): management level
*$p < .05$, **$p < .01$, ***$p < .001$.

Table A2: Principal axis factoring analyses of latent variables

	Teachers				Principals			
	M	SD	Factor score	Cronbach's alpha	M	SD	Factor score	Cronbach's alpha
Organizational commitment (affective)	70.10	25.32		0.75	83.90	24.21		0.69
I do not feel emotionally attached to the school.	3.77	1.13	0.65		4.28	1.17	0.64	
I do not have a strong sense of belonging to the school	3.84	1.14	0.65		4.44	1.04	0.64	
Transformational leadership *As a leader I…/My principal…*	51.79	25.32		0.90	79.35	12.94		0.79
…provide(s) a compelling vision of the organization's future.	3.15	1.11	0.80		4.15	0.65	0.59	
…articulate(s) and generate(s) enthusiasm for a shared vision and mission.	3.03	1.11	0.87		4.22	0.59	0.70	
…facilitate(s) the acceptance of common goals for the school.	2.99	1.07	0.88		4.15	0.68	0.75	
…say(s) things that make employees proud to be part of the organization.	3.12	1.14	0.83		4.21	0.71	0.71	
Management by reward *As a leader I…/My principal…*	37.72	25.32		0.85	68.21	21.47		0.75
…reward(s) my employees' performance (e.g. through wage supplements), when they live up to expectations.	2.55	1.17	0.72		3.77	0.99	0.69	
…reward(s) the employees dependent on how well they perform their jobs.	2.47	1.02	0.72		3.69	0.93	0.70	
Management by exception	33.46	22.91		0.51	38.62	23.16		0.63
…focus(es) attention on irregularities, mistakes, exceptions and deviations from what is expected of me.	2.54	1.16	0.49		2.18	1.00	0.56	
…dismiss teachers, if they over a longer period do not perform satisfactory.	2.14	1.07	0.48		2.92	1.16	0.59	

Note: Oblimin rotated

REFERENCES

Argys, L., Rees, D., and Brewer, D. (1996): "Detracking America's Schools: Equity and Zero Cost?", *Journal of Policy Analysis and Management,* 15(4): 623–645

Angle, H. L. & Perry, J. L. (1981): "An empirical assessment of organizational commitment and organizational effectiveness", *Administrative Science Quarterly,* 26:1-14

Avolio, B. J., W. Zhu, W. Koh, & P. Bhatia (2004): "Transformational leadership and organizational commiment: Mediating role of psychological empowerment and moderating role of structural distance". *Journal of Organizational Behavior,* 25 (8): 951–968

Balfour, D. L., & Wechsler, B. (1996): "Organizational commitment: Antecedents and outcomes in public organizations", *Public Productivity and Management Review,* 19(3): 256-277

Bass, B. M. (1990): "From Transactional to Transformational Leadership: Learning to Share the Vision", *Organizational Dynamics,* Winter: 19-31

Bass, B.M. (1985). *Leadership and performance beyond expectations.* New York: Free Press

Bozeman, B. (2000). *Bureaucracy and red tape.* Upper Saddle Hill, NJ: Prentice Hall

Buchanan, B. (1974): "Building organizational commitment: The socialization of managers in work organizations", *Administrative Science Quarterly,* 19: 533-546

Burns, J. M. (1978). *Leadership.* New York: Harper & Row

Christensen. T., Per Lægreid, Paul G. Roness & Kjell Arne Røvik (2009). *Organisasjonsteori for offentlig sektor.* Oslo: Universitetsforlaget

Christensen,J. G. & Pallesen, Thomas (2009): "Public Employee trends and the organization of public sector tasks", in *The State at Work: Comparative Public Service Systems.* red. Hans-Ulrich Derlien; B. Guy Peters. Vol. 2 Cheltenham: Edward Elgar Publishing, Incorporated, 2009: 7-33

Chun, Y. H., & Rainey, H. G. (2005): "Goal ambiguity in U.S. federal agencies", *Journal of Public Administration Research and Theory,* 15(1): 1-30

Cohen, A. (2003): "Multiple commitments in the workplace: An integrative approach", Mawah, NJ: Lawrence Erlbaum

Hambrick, D.C. & P. A. Mason (1984): "Upper Echelons: The Organization as a Reflection of Its Top Managers", *The Academy of Management Review,* 9 (2): 193-206

Henderson, V., Miezkowski, P., and Sauvageau, Y. (1978): "Peer Group Effects and Educational Production Functions", *Journal of Public Economics,* 10: 97–106

Klein, Howard J., Molloy, Janice C. and Brinsfield, Chad T. (2012): "Re-conceptualizing workplace commitment to redress a stretched construct: Revisiting assumptions and removing confounds", *Academy of Management,* 37(1): 130-151

Kline, C., & Peters, L. (1990): "Behavioral commitment and tenure of new employees: A replication and extension", *Academy of Management,* 34: 194-204

Latham, gary P., Borgogni, Laura, and Petitta, Laura (2008): "Goal Setting and performance Management in the Public Sector", *International Public Management Journal,* 11(4): 385-403

Mathieu, J. E., and Zajac, D. M. (1990): "A review and meta-analysis of the antecedents, correlates, and consequences of organizational commitment", *Psychological Bulletin,* 108: 171–194

Meyer, J. W. and Rowan, B. (1977): "Institutional organizations: formal structure as myth and ceremony," *American Journal of Sociology,* 83: 340-63

Meyer, J.P. and Allen, N.J. (1991): "A Tree-component conceptualization of organizational commitment", *Human Resource Management Review,* 1: 61-89

Meyer, J. P., Allen, N. J., and Smith, C. A. (1993): "Commitments to organizations and occupations: Extension and test of a three component conceptualization", *Journal of Applied Psychology,* 78: 538–551

Meyer, J. P., and Allen, N. J. (1997). *Commitment in the workplace: Theory, research, and application.* Thousand Oaks, CA: Sage

Meyer, J. P., and Herscovitch, L. (2001): "Commitment in the work- place: Toward a general model", *Human Resource Management Review,* 11: 299–326

Meyer, J. P., Stanley, D. J., Herscovitch, L., and Topolnytsky, L. (2002): "Affective, continuance, and normative commitment to the organization: A meta-analysis of antecedents, correlates, and consequences", *Journal of Vocational Behavior,* 61: 20–52

Mowday, R. T., Steers, R. M., and Porter, L. W. (1979): "The measurement of organizational commitment", *Journal of Vocational Behavior,* 14: 224–247

O'Reilly, C., & Caldwell, D. (1980): "Job choice: The impact of intrinsic and extrinsic factors on subsequent satisfaction and commitment", *Journal of Applied Psychology,* 65: 559-565

O'Toole, J. Laurence Jr. and Meier, Kenneth J. (2011). *Public Management. Organizations, Governance, and Performance*. Cambridge

Park, Sung M. & Rainey, Hal G. (2007): "Antecedents, Mediators, and Consequences of Affective, Normative, and Continuance Commitment: Empirical Tests of Commitment Effects in Federal Agencies", *Review of Public Personnel Administration*, 27 (3): 197-226

Pandey, S. K., & Rainey, H. G. (2006): "Public managers' perceptions of organizational goal ambiguity: Analyzing alternate models", *International Public Management Journal*, 9(2), 85-112

Perry, J. L., & Rainey, H. G. (1988): "The public-private distinction in organizational theory: A critique and research strategy", *Academy of Management Review*, 13, 182-201

Porter, Lyman W., William J. Crampon & Frank J. Smith (1976): "Organizational Commitment and Managerial Turnover: A Longitudinal Study", *Organizational Behavior and Human Performance*, 15: 87-98

Rainey, H. G. (2009). *Understanding and Managing Public Organizations*. John Wiley & Sons, 4th edition

Rainey, H.G. and P. Steinbauer (1999): "Galloping Elephants: Developing Elements of a Theory of Effective Government Organizations", *Journal of Public Administration Research and Theory*, 9(1): 1–3

Salancik, G. (1977): "Commitment and the control of organizational behavior and belief", in Shaw, B.M. and Salancik, G.R. (Eds.), *New Directions in Organizational Behavior*, St Clare Press, Chicago, IL, 123-35

Schein, Edgar H. (1992). *Organizational Culture and Leadership*. 2nd edition, San Francisco: Jossey-Bass

Scott, R. W. (2008). *Institutions and Organizations. Ideas and Interests.* London: Sage Publications

Scott, R. W. and Gerald F. Davis (2007). *Organizations and Organizing, Rational, Natural, and Open System Perspectives*. New Jersey: Pearson Education

Selznick, Philip (1948): "Foundations of the Theory of Organization", *American Sociology Review*, 13: 25-35

Sollinger, O. N, van Olffen, W. & Roe, R. A. (2008): "Beyond the three-component model of organizational commitment", *Journal of Applied Psychology*, 93(1): 70-83

Summers, A., and Wolfe, B. (1977): "Do Schools Make a Difference?", *American Economic Review*, 67: 639–52

Stazyk, E. C., Panday, S. K. & B. E. Wright (2011): "Understanding Affective Organizational Commitment: The Importance of Institutional Context", *The American review of Public Administration*, 41: 603-624

Stazyk, E. C., & Goerdel, H. T. (2011): "The benefits of bureaucracy: Public managers' perceptions of political support, goal ambiguity, and organizational effectiveness", *Journal of Public Administration Research and Theory*, 21 (4): 645-672

Steinhaus, Carol S. & Perry, James L. (1996): "Organizational Commitment: Does Sector Matter?", *Public Productivity & Management Review*, 19 (3): 278-288

Stevens, J. M., J. M. Beyer, & H. M. Trice (1978): "Assessing personal, role, and organizational predictors of managerial commitment", *Academy of Management journal*, 21 (3): 380–396

Suchman, Mark C. (1995): "Managing Legitimacy: Strategic and Institutional Approaches", *Academy of Management Review*, 20(3): 571-610

Warwick, D. P., Meade, M., & Reed, T. (1975). *A theory of public bureaucracy*. Cambridge, MA: Harvard University Press.

Wilson, James Q. (1989). *Bureaucracy. What Government Agencies do and Why They do it*. BasicBooks

Wright, Bradley E. (2004): "The Role of Work Context in Work Motivation: A Public Sector Application of Goal and Social Cognitive Theories", *Journal of Public Administration Research and Theory*, 14(1): 59-78

Wright, T. A. & D. G. Bonett (2002): "The moderating effects of employee tenure on the relation between organizational commitment and job performance: A meta-analysis", *Journal of Applied Psychology,* 87 (6): 1183

Wright, B. E., Moynihan, D. P. &S. K. Pandey (2012): "Pulling the Levers: Transformational Leadership, Public Service Motivation, and Mission Valence", *Public Administration Review* 72(2): 206–215